D0298049

Under the Blue Moon

WITHDRAWN
IOWA STATE UNIVERSITY
LIBRARY

UNDER
THE
BLUE
MOON

Poems by

J. T. Barbarese

The University
of Georgia Press
Athens and London

© 1985 by J. T. Barbarese
Published by the University of Georgia Press
Athens, Georgia 30602

All rights reserved

Set in 10 on 13 Linotron 202 Gill Sans

The paper in this book meets the guidelines for
permanence and durability of the Committee on
Production Guidelines for Book Longevity of the
Council on Library Resources.

Printed in the United States of America

89 88 87 86 85   5 4 3 2 1

Library of Congress Cataloging in Publication Data
Barbarese, J. T.
    Under the blue moon.

    I. Title. PS3552.A59178U5 1985   811'.54   85-5880
ISBN 0-8203-0801-3 (alk. paper)
ISBN 0-8203-0802-1 (pbk. : alk. paper)

Nature
Touz jors martele, touz jors forge,
Touz jors ses pieces renovele
Par generacion novele.

—*Jean de Meun*

The publication of this book is supported by a grant from the National Endowment for the Arts, a federal agency.

Acknowledgments

Acknowledgment is made to the following journals in which some of the poems in this volume were first published:

The Smith: "Mnemosyne"
Carolina Quarterly: "Joseph," "That Last Spring"
Indiana Review: "Through the Sunshower Off Stage Point"
Denver Quarterly: "Sunshine"

Contents

I

II

III

IV

I

Dusk

—as for the starlings
they seem to condense
right out of the dusk
here on the window
like checks or square roots that
run south to north
fully the distance
light travels the sprawl
of the complex's shadow
over the cornfield
where they uproot the pasture's
harvest of worms
risen bisected
like this loop of bellwire
pigtailed and tangled
up in my arm. Now
I'm repeating the thing
just as I see it
and each time I do
changing the ending—

Mnemosyne

Patience, she warned me,
there's a dangerous air
to everything today
and it bothers you, as if where-
ever you look things look away
and commence a history

apart from you. Is the sky
the result of your looking at it?
What you see there a screen
through which clouds have been
ascending like credits?
It's only you and I,

our appearances, projections,
ascensions you are seeing,
not the incomparable brilliance
of April and its entering
into sad association
with the moon in the distance.

What darkness cannot mediate
it skips. So separate her face
from the oval teeming with birds,
the birds from their space and their space
from whatever you have measured
across a likeness, separate

the distance from the moon
and what it carries to the sea
in its silverness, to leave out there
whatever you're meant to be.

See how the asters bow the air.
Ignore the illusion

of a seamless finality
where the moon's changes cease
and your eyes rest in your head.
Patience, she told me,
the quince is turning red,
the air is luscious with bees.

Occupation

(for Ken Watson)

The bines of the willows brush over the ground
like intravenous needles. Trailers snake through
      the outcropped shales
and limestones, the donated granite, and descending
blackbirds play over the scene like hands
but it's still a perfect blank, an unsettled thing
that keeps leading the eye to the pale blond sun,
      indistinct, a smudge on the daylight,

a scar of vaccination.
The eye moves through it like fire, occupying,
campaigning and probing for details that ebb and flow,
      stretched out of shape like the sun and easily
floating like bright forms on the skin of a bubble
until something happens. The telephone rings.
A pump goes on automatically. Water
rushes to water. A letter that tells
a story like this, though unmailed, gets to

a destination. Detained in occupied countries,
admiring cows out in pastures, the admonishing sky,
the shape of his head in a pond, all the carrier knows
is that he bears more than he reads, and in private
he admits what he knows keeps dividing, division being
the mind's mathematics for solving the world
      that arrives too late in spring
or after the carrier's gone. No time for letters,
      no time for shapes conferred on the distance

whose silhouettes carry meaning. No word on events
that come like April rain and only wet the ground,

which is our only understanding. But jokes get made,
and familiars retreat like puns into the formal circle
        of language to tell you
what can be done and what is undoing the circle:
pink trees the thickening
mustard of sunlight on brick the heads bobbing back and
forth—

it's like those engravings
of Bull Run. Picnickers up the hill
above the encampments, girls in shining brocade
playing with willow bines that stray into their eyes
        and turning slowly away
to the plums spread on the grass just as a bellnote
gets lost in golden gunfire and the sun fills with smoke
pigtailing down to the fight, and a name

is pulled from the roll. The carriage bell's report
        echoes here, then it doesn't.
Perfect blankness, Watson. Then the flight of the blackbirds
squirting out of the dogwoods into contentious noon.

Thaw

It's shown me that all knowing is
recovery from really clear vision:

the melting of ice bears out some force
unpeeling the glass from the dazzle

as six-sided coldness comes unstuck and slips
out of flakes into raindrops the light grips

then smears down the space
covered with sunniness.

False spring down on the pavement
thaws noontime into puddles tangent,

weirdly, to all but puddles
as though that's where they settle

those moments of all-dazzlement
uncorked from the sun—

neither sight nor sense
but a moment that runs like this pane of glass

with its wet flakes, and its yield of beads,
and its raindrops signing this pane of glass like a deed.

A Remark You Made

(for Peter Heimlich)

You are just crossing the window.
The weather is starting to clear.
Something inside catches your eye,
I think a cloud, and you go on to say

something strange about how we relate
better to what we remember than what we are
as the bad ice-storm passed through. It left
the weather clear, the sky runny with clouds

and soft color; it drew those remarks from you
just as you passed the bay window
when your arm dropped and your voice fell down
the scale and stopped

at words I can't quite remember.
There, you said, pointing out;
your voice filled with noisy music.
Rising, then strangled mid-octave,

an airbrake moans through the snow.
This window's a score of bright blotches,
zeroes of ice, hatchings of nails.
Like a G clef a cat

squats in the blinds.
If only I could see what I hear
now you'd be crossing this window
here—right here.

Going South

Everything here, the time passed,
hasn't passed, it's just happened again.
What I leave behind is a stand-in
future copied and propped up like skrim.
Dreamy starlings cover floodplains
beating their wings in dust

while bright mechanical thunderstorms
chase us up and back, rehearsed
confusion. But the real one
is passing out of reach of each of us.
What I'll recall is the sun's shining
and rising and setting each morning

as though some mad hope
kept it blundering into the daylight.
I'll keep thinking of sunlight beating
down through the hawks
over Chickie's Rock, high on the heat,
and how the sun runs south in the Susquehanna then loops

up and off with the river, as though great fear
kept it blundering out of my sight.
Feel it pulling away from us,
entering awful eclipses,
blundering back out at night.
Mixed up with the moon on the shore.

Sunshine

"It never looks like an accident.
You look around and what's everyday
gets caught up in rag-man's song
and carried like that carries along
hard, common things in worked-out ways.
What's everyday is self-evident—

sunshine, hummingbirds, me, dawn,
the clouds balled up like laundry,
the shanty towns, dead moths on the floor.
It's the sound stuck to things everywhere.
What you want is to strip the sound away
and fill with your noise what I hear."

Yes, it's my cheap little overture
that dogs you into the corded sheet
of sunshine spread over the floor,
and it's me who foxes the conversation,
and the air is hot with my presence,
and today is fixed by my seeming
the thematic root of your being.
No, the hard part is that being is dense
and gets in the way of the sunshine.

Katherine Wallace

You were in and out of the parlor, serving.
You were filling glasses and pauses, you,
as though mending it, let the conversation
run from the darkened deck-chairs and sudden rain
to you, the transitional figure, he said,
slumped over his drink. Right at that moment
the smoke grafted to the sunlight went into eclipse
and the whole room verged on death when you,
tossing your head back, roared out at him,
walked to my chair, whispered, your lips by mine,
your body doubled to me and your rising hand
closing my vision of all of them all bent to listen.

That Last Spring

"I couldn't really tell.
There was an early moonrise.
She puzzled through the grass
and sunflowers spiking up like brass
wheels outshining from in back
the rosebushes she picked through
without picking a single one.
She said now look at that moon,
now look at all this,
fat and greasy with us.
Hooked like a fish,
she said, kneeling in grass.
And I watched it struggle up
climbing the light into dark
and fulvous, muddied dusk,
isinglass smeared with stars.
It got higher and higher. It climbed.
It coiled around her knotted legs
right up to her fists, her nails and throat—
come on, she said, kneeling in the grass,
smeared with the egg
of the dandelions."

Girl Who Got in the Way

A bizarre partnership: you grinned, she grinned back
but the horizon got my attention—a muzzle expelling
too many starlings to see swept into the southwest
and South Carolina, anywhere south of Durham—

of you, kicking your way through weeds and trash
and clouds of moths while the evening foreshortened
the shiny cars lined up like tureens in a row
in Winn-Dixie's parking lot. Your paths crossed
and clouds of them you kicked out of your way

filled it. You picked them off with your hat.
She paddled the air to you and the dog snapped at air
and the two of you traded grins. Thunder over bells
came through the door right behind her. In that early dark
the moths fried in the breezeway's recessed lights.

Before it got dark came the grayed-out time when they thrived.
The air was theirs for a while. Then the starlings
tossed into the sundown like fistfuls of pepper
usurped the distance
and the air was shapely, free of moths. Then she passed
you climbing a path with a dog snapping at nothing. . . .

That fast it was over. How the rain pits a dirt path
got my attention. Then the bells, then the thunder
came out of her mouth better than any of this.
More usurping shapeliness, that fast it was over.
I stepped over drifts of them, leaving.

That Summer

That summer seemed staged. Driving, I remembered
her hand shaping a sand form. Bosomy gulls,
stark and attentive, stood into the wind. The sea
and the peal of her voice over dreamy sea-thunder.
The emotional burst was complete. Her fear was gone.
Some ship's single sail biting too much horizon.

It was the drive, eight hours, that brought up the horizon
but as showy, as staged. Like the long-remembered
scene on the edge of the bed. Eyes that are never gone
long, but come back as biplanes. Laughing gulls
parked by the sand forms. A background of thunder,
her unintentional voice. Crack of the sea.

The whole thing shakes out, comes uncreased, the sea, even,
reshaping the brutalized shore before the horizon's
blue vacancies, a stately funhouse of thunder.
That too came and went like a thing I remembered
as the frame of all this. Then skyfuls of gulls.
The road-lines, like hyphens. A horn, blown and gone.

Commerce

You walked around in circles just as I got to work
the morning we got to the shore. If all that was a dream
then my present is waking up. This is city daylight
where a figure gets lost in his lines and the lines get rid
of themselves if you wait long enough, people go walking
around a block with their dogs, but not around lawns.

Things stop dead on corners. This morning that lawn
straightened out into Mercy Street and I went to work.
I got in line with the other sleepwalkers walking
in terror of dawn because dawn dawns on dreams
and brutally undreams them. Dawn it was that rid
me of my dreams by working them out in the light

coldly unpuzzling all sorts of walks in the daylight.
Love never entered the thing. I forgot the lawn,
how you got up early and walked around to get rid
of a nightmare while I buried myself in some work.
It fled like light into day. Just like you in that dream
that drove you out of me, I had to start walking.

It felt like a tour through a ruin, or sleepwalking
past lots and some bum's ring of stones in the early light.
Only the dawn rose suddenly, solving that dream.
It changed the morning by changing the lawn.
The situation worked out because I went to work
like a normal Joe, wanting nothing except to get rid

of you and even me. I know that was how you rid
your nightmare of me that April. You began walking
through daylight awake, alone and alive to the work
of big, godly forces that live despite me in the light

that hung like a flag from the sun, ankle-high in the lawn
bedded thick with marigolds. Dawn burned down the dream.

I got up and went to the window, sick of dreams
and realized you would not live here. Then I got rid
of your few remains. It was like weeding a lawn.
I think of you now and then when I see women walking
in circles, or wake up blind in the city daylight
and watch the dawn stretching out people going to work.

Dawn undreams itself. Daylight goes walking
like a ghost looking for darkness. Light goes to light,
weeds make lawns into lots and lots go to work.

Low Tragic

Your eyes belong to a man haunted
by the wrong past. It's not even mine.
This complicates you with a nobleness strange
because mistaken. Still, whatever you do,
may you see what your innocence looks like now
that another voice spells out the power
you still say is yours.

Stars by the Moon

You have buried your self in what's not you,
so what's left except what's here?
Your face fills with other faces
encroaching on your open reflection
and is blended into the world. Their eyes
cloud the sudsed-up green of your eyes
and your eyes get lost, but lost as sound,
not as light gets lost.
Lean into yourself.
The stars cluster around you like punks around pools
contaminated by time, never by you.

Your Name

I spoke and it escaped me.
Breath on a tool, a coin, a key,
on a plane, glass, on the hand-polished poles
of trolleycars etched with names,
breath out in the cold
unshaping gale
for one second
held it before me.

White Fire

Lost in the wind, your voice took shape
and just as fast it lost it.
Cold returned and healed the air.
What did I have to give you?
I held your hand
and you led me over
the pond that fell apart for us.
You dragged me in, sucking my name
back out of the wind

and somewhere out in your dad's pastures
Duchess heaved and shook her mane
and blew white fire out.

II

Hymn at Holy Cross Cemetery

Missa Solemnis

"Nothing that hurts us hurts him now!
The dogs bark at our trespassing steps
and children without futures grow
like storms bluffing rain, and blow by.
Now we pick our way into what he was.
Six rose bushes bent like barnyard cocks,
a poker deck. He has become all of us

and things that are stuck hard to their names,
and all shall someday come unstuck before God.
Now we mourn the way he did, heading for mass,
we stop by the house and how quickly we pass
this thing that's so still, laid out at home.
Today, his street pillared with lindens,
shaking down golden dust on our hair,
with his name in our systems we walk alone

and names alone tell us all that we know.
But shall we live on, only to die?
The distance between our lives and our God's
goodness is here to the graves—the dirt.
His past is what we are trapped in, friends,
when we name God we shorten the distance to go,
we grow into our deaths throughout our futures,
and death, isn't death our futures? Death?"

Watch how we smoke in the dark vestibules:
we speak the smoke first, then suck in a breath.
Breath is like dawn, one more victory,
but noon comes and turns the sky down, like a quilt.

25

The poorbox looks quilled with our cigarettes.
Big things blast in the distance.
Kids without a life blur by.
On corners the dogs howl after.

Humanity

"Under the fatal hill it's dark.
Beyond the stone is a stand of trees.
They shine like whetted knives until
the moon sets. When the sun breaks out
stars fall through its hole and the darkness leaves
only clouds, like worn-through spots in quilts,
for the sun to stick its white face through.

Then the dark and the moon come back, again,
and the buried stars rise up, again,
and the sun shatters the darkness again,
and the clouds quilt it into a daytime again,

but that man is dead and he won't come back.
A man is born, he dies, he doesn't come back."

Contact

"But what do they think I am, an angel?
Do these people who eat Jesus Christ every day
eat a regular meal? This man's got to eat.
It's a good day when you can eat, a bad day when you can't.
All I see is flowers. I don't see no food.
I know what I know. Life is like food.
When your food has filled all the holes in your life,

your life craps you out. Then you fill up a hole
and it starts again. You got something better?"

*

"But you'd be surprised what's hid in just junk,
them funky fishcrates and them knotty pine boards.
You drill them knots out of number two pine,
they smell good in your hand, like parsley, or money,
then putty them up, you make a spicerack.
A typical spicerack you get out of a fruitcrate
goes as high as a deuce on Ninth Street. The work gets me high.
You rub pine till it's shiny like oilstone
and the second you see your eyes, you're all done."

*

"Old ladies smell bad. Between perfume and tears
it's like piss on old track shoes. Then they lift the tears up
on their pinkies, like pearls, and suck on the pinkies. . . .
When this one here talks, it's like burning leaves. *Strong.*
The burny smell comes out right when she talks.
Look, look what she does with the pinkie. . . .
When she finally shuts up, I'll pay my respects.
I still don't see food. You see any food?"

Despair

"The organizing spider
organized all day
and when she organized her web
she kicked herself away

and strung out far on a shiny thread
of web pearled with rain

she organized and organized
and organized again—"

Passage

Through the rosettes in the roof
the light passes and stains the aisles
then creeps through the ranks of candles far
into the crèche where a raised slipper
is caught toeing the world.
The sun breasts the tiled roof.

The sun drops off to nowhere
and it's warmer in candlelight.
The streetlamp on my bare hands will
make mountains of my knuckles.
I'll want to be out here tonight.
To feel the cold air.

Dust

Dust pioneers the sun's fast
resurgence down a telescoping
cone of the afternoon's resilience
peeled back in a burst

and through the breach comes
lots more dust
bound in a tight beam herding
dust to dust and light to light

to the spot where the settling stuff
crowds out over the earth
and probes the patent
seamlessness of all surfaces.

Hymn at Holy Cross Cemetery

"He will die an endless death,
he will die an endless dying.
Into the roots and the smoothed-out grasses
he will die, and always be dying.
Underfoot, beneath your heels,
he'll rise to the ancient death.
Nobody's breath will not taste of him,
no summer will smell and not smell of him, of the grass and the sap of
    his sweat.
He will die an endless death,
his death will always be rising
into skin, sky, wind, the hot rain
on these stones and smoothed-out grasses.
His death will be as endless
as the winds under the high sky.
His eyes will be gravel, his lips will be sprouts,
his nerves will be saplings, his nails will be leaves,
his skin will be arteried by the tiniest
creepers and climbers, his mind tunneled through
by the worms, his thoughts, as they think his death through
like a puzzle over and over again,
that his breath may go up into the life
of the rainclouds, and be blown back as sweet wind,
that his beard be stubble over the pebbles
whose sheen holds the sunlight close to his face,
whose warmth makes the moonlight warm.
He will die his endless death,
he will grow into your lives patiently.
You will wipe your feet of him at your doors,
wash your hands of him when you eat,
breathe him out on your pillowcases, but
you'll never be rid of him, not at all,
as he endlessly dies back into your life."

The Waters

I have nothing in my hands
now despite my fingers' shaping
something that they had
once, the very first
things lost to me, small hollows

I press and ring awake,
I yield asleep. At noon
I knelt down to the frozen tracks
night cast and noon was lighting
but ice-locked they kept me waiting

like the dog that stalled above them
whose water they became, whose shape
they held. I wanted them at noon,
the waters held me there but I
knew beforehand that they would

not be held, would not hold.

III

Dawn

I'm not what they say I am
when they call me by a name
cobbled out of memory or
raked off the last generation
and some old lady's Bible. I am
not the one they say I am
in the morning when my risen
flesh adds nothing to the dark
but blots across the walls and windows
the little dawn that draws today
out on a skinny hope to add
just this, my own addition, to
the light, my dark "today."
I add nothing to your morning
but what I got at evening—
a shadow here, my own warm breath
sucked back through my teeth
as though life spat me up.
Not the name they gave me,
not what the name says,
I add what I come on.

The Flow of the Grain

The flow of the grain is a muddy frieze
on the door. All gold and shallow browns
one edge seems to have snagged something
blue—sky through tent-poles. Or sails

pressed on the sky. All that I know
is my breath breaking against the sheets,
a migrating speech of fever become
sweat, delerium, song. I'm just a guest.

Earth is the sensible drunken host.
Beneath the baseboard piled dust
is what, the earth says, is left. Breath's
hoot and rah on my flesh: hot wind, cold water.

Through the Sunshower Off Stage Point

I see you, swaying under a lamp,
your eyes buggy with salt and wind,
the sockets quarries of shadow.
From the master's thick neck the glass swings
studded with rain. You point;
he stares where you point. I hear gaslamps
hissing, the crack of the sea on the keel,
the waves sucked down the hull. I see
space scooped out of the faraway land
all lit up: rocks uncovered,
a woman, the wagon road
that leads to Stage Point, raspy with gravel
trod by doctors and wives, that swamp
behind it and the road out
and the graveyard yellow and wild
with bullfrogs torn from their shadows.
Tourists are chasing little charts
blown over the rocks. In the downpour
the sun-splattered stone shines violently
in the sunshower's moment and I see
you through the tissues of storm,
the drowned one who grins for good.

Loud jacks turret the sky down here,
a place of rods and rivets. Nothing
heals the distances between this and that:
walk down some fire-bombed, noisy spot
and you're less scared than awed. Up there,
spars of chimneys front the antennas
swaying like crosstrees in the wind
shaped out of dust and kicking up
as it wails down the iron steps to the street.

A bottle breaks. A door slams,
a kid loses childhood in one blow
and a thousand ragged starlings perched
in your empty house empty out
and head south in broken formation.

Joseph

Get yourself out of there
the world runs otherwise, the river
doesn't run there anymore go
look for it   The seventh shore
uncreased at last beneath me, sloping
up while the river ran away. We walked
down the bank quickly, kicking clouds
of perfumes from the undergrowth
smeared with his steps before me
and smelling the far side of the bank
before seeing him. Then I
heard him shout to me *Goodbye*
and turned to a level, perfect plain
like *no* flat in front of me for
I was there. Walking forth
hands at his side he stopped
and I saw the other shores again,
creased, sloped, whiter than milk,
a long bright spray winding out to him,
like the stretch of his shadow that begins
here, with one arm suddenly rising,
his head suddenly turning away,
that arm caught in a half-wave and then
sliding back into the shadows that lead
him who got me down the hill
back where the river runs and it runs
perfectly, as it never will
reflected in faces, filled with voices
filling its thronging score, a crisp
and gentle rampage it runs and runs
assembled out of this and that,
this wind, this water, this light,

it runs and rose like the sun inside me
as though the shore you sought seeks you,
finds you looking. Walking out
he waved and the wind caught the full of his sleeve
and whopped as it rippled over
the concatenated waters. He
said *Here*
          his face turned sunward
raising his left hand, dropping his right,
to the river that gained on, then gained me,
and stripped I struck the chilling wave
and naked he called me

Night

Under the clouds the appearing world
is what the priests once called it,

God's dreams set down in prose,
but the world known way earlier

is out there where the shadows are striking out
from the light's slowly massing posse. Heading west

unborn, they wait on a name:
night, say, comes in the space dusk makes.

A fretwork of lightning over the homes
surrounds the shadows like leading.

I have done it all backwards but I have done it:

the past is mine first,
then the past is past.

III

"And so it is a man can be made to
disappear, like a thought unfinished

like one word not followed

follow me follow me
into the morning. Light
dawns and claims the horizon
it grips like sound in a brazen horn
and calls between wall and wall

follow me follow me
back to acting. Coming
out of the hill that rots
into the flowers that's not
a gaping monster just me

at the end of the series
followed by nothing
present or future. Life
has evacuated the dead and their dying notes
stay fixed like flags at distances
where the roofs grow fences rooted

in walls staggering on
word on word, follow me follow me
towering up and past sameness and distance
out of it

till I am out of it"

Right After Sleep

It looks like peaches in the glass. The shades'
whiteness slowly bleaches all that daily

sun spent on a window that night,
like a credit, succeeds, holds tight.

Light like rust to iron clings to the glass
as if the glass were facing day too much,

night too much to face. Watching, I'm unsure,
holding the world away, seeing it assemble

like the old one, seeing it get brighter.
The sun treads leafy shade.

A Review of the Thing

Some light gets loose, some light slips
around a pebble, snubs it, holds it down.

How black in the sunlight the glass looks! The hours
feel like locks on the sunshine, and maybe that's why

these pebbly lots look like the sun's headstones.
Light comes and dies here. Heaped in gravel

day runs out of the hole that night leaves
and lands broken and shot. Do I have

no shape except for the shapes up there
in the angles of sunny windows? They're not me.

Dinky faces framed in the windows like shots
on a blotter, they're not mine, the clatter of pebbles

underfoot, that's not mine, sunshine hanging down
rotting holes in the haze isn't mine

but the broken glass, how the broken glass

holds its reflected moment up
for the second I stop to look—that's mine.

Street Scene

"We used to set up a cardboard box on the ground.
The box was Camelot. The ground was blacktop.
There were no deer in the distance, just Girard Park.
The park looked painted. I thought it was England."
The horror: the stone dropped down the well
never clucked, never hit the sides, ever.

The Horses on Broad Street

At dawn they're evenly bedded
down on the islands, the braces racked up
and ravelled like duckblind on the unshipped
yellow legs. The cops whip them up
and old and wooden they are led
thirty-some blocks up Broad Street

propping up drunks, mummers, the cops,
past the ragged brownstones and blinds
snapped up and down while the whole city
stands behind them and they're walked north
in that perfect, frozen formation.

Ronny Smash's America

"I was on one knee under one of them trees
down The Lakes last Saturday
and I'm bending like this to empty my shoes
of the stones and the sticks and the leaves
when all of a sudden I'm hearing this hiss
and the fighters are on top of me:
I mean wing after wing of F-105's
and in back, that fat C-130
everybody's seen except me
and then the Chinooks, like bald old men
just killing time, pausing to see
the tops of the cracking towers
and the flames from the refinery
then a Cessna came winding it out real loud
under one wing of the jets
and then the moon a little lost-looking
and then like right out of the trees

birds: all these birds went shooting up
with a crack like a blowout straight up
making big sky-wheels, big fat circles,
like hoops with the centers on me,
big bullseyes, big rodeo ropes
that can tie the sky to the trees
and drag the clouds right into your shoes
full of stones, sticks, and leaves."

Love

Watch him, squatting there beside
the seam where the lawn hits the blacktop
and the veronica seeks the grass
like a fallen frontier;

or there, in that bed of clover
he mounts like a magic rug
while he browns in his twelfth summer
beside weeds, sun-darkened and dying.

As he sleeps, the lights outdoors
make lanes in the night that spreads west
like a wake from Maury's front door;
I have to get us out of here
before the veronica is gone
and borders are all I know.

Brick

That square of brick pushed
like a black thumb through the weeds
killed them—or the weeds, lacking light,
in the shade of the brick grew dwarfed

as they grew up around it—
just a brick. And it punched
a hole in the lot
where all that junk

lay bunched or gathered
for burning or nothing
I know of. Itself,
it's the lot's sole monument

to what holds the rest of us here
to Mercy Street's heaped-up promise.
As patient as gods, on the steps,
men smoke, men stare. Smoke is spring's monument

sucked from nothing but dry, lewd dusk.
I'm going out after that brick: it's mine.
It's no more theirs than or the lot's than the marks
their cigarettes leave on the steps

or my thumb leaves on this page.

Promises

Certain big promises
never come down to earth, to us.
Like the smell of rain
they hide in the wind,

and the way winds hide in the clouds
men do down here. Down here they grow
giants that don't go down,
hard, unkillable, heaped-up and pure

unbreakable promises. But how could they know
such hard, unbreakable patience
if they didn't know how to use the body,
if they didn't live in its every square inch?

Hands up, feet planted square,
facing what's there like the stones
that stick from the weeds that grow all seasons
and hold the little light that gets down this far.

Brother to Brother

"Or what about that midnight I
jumped off that boat, breaking my hand
lunging for the dock? Whose surer
hands, before she ran at me
rising on the floodtide, heaved?
Or our voices, bark to pith,
pitched seamlessly to Marylou,
sun comes up bloodred?" Listen.
The frozen wind just raked the street-
and starlight on the windshield, see?
So shut up, let the damn thing be,
poised like dawn, ready to break.
"No. Your voice may be the only one
that's not become a caption, your hands
the other pair I count on now.
I never knew what you meant to me
until I missed the dock." Let's say
I saw tonight way ahead of time.
I felt the brute inconsequence
of talk, piss in a snowstorm.
I smelled graveyard heather, birch in the wind.
The waves look like smiles painted on.
The steeples look like duncecaps.
Who else but you would get this?

Playground

(for Crow)

Now and then it comes to rest
and hard dark eyes are on what happened
once before me, and half in darkness.
You are flushed out of night like distance

from moonlight, sad but safe.
I climb and stuff a rim, a bent halo,
hard lights strike a boned beast,
the monkey bars. But all this mess

is shapelessness made a stand-in.
The bitch next door just whacked her baby.
The baby's yelp is what's back there—
mortal attention wounded by everything

about to come. This bitch is hooked
on the sight of her chest in a windshield,
biting the air her baby mugs
for the snapshot that's never been taken,

and over the sands and over the lots
the moon comes, dragging more past.
The baby keeps biting the air
and the wind bites right back.

Mercy Street

Open your eyes. All at once the sky
rebounds like the sky off the water the day

before light got scattered like dust and stars
got stuck in the glass in the street. Either

the eyes are making this up or the mind
does its best thinking off to one side

and without looking up. When the snow is like this,
lying like scrim fallen onto the set,

who knows what's made up? Like milk
white in the backhoe's bucket the drifts

reflect so candidly on the side
streets I close my eyes

to back into what you were:
clouds in my mirror the moment before

like a flip-book show the window rose
and the cold rushed in and the clouds

defrosted. There was still the sun.
It shone hard on the flashing under the sash

for a long time, but not forever. Impossible that
you be coextensive with what this street

reflects? You pop from the set of all sets
and adjust your godliness blindingly, being

my way back to what you were: a hard-working huckster-god,
ungodded by winter, by merciless ices.

I still don't trust what's here. It might just be
held in this bubble of history like those lights

that time on the waves' little peaks. These drifts
creep into peaks and each peak

is gravity-chamfered. The cinderblock wall
is reshaped by the still sacred wind

and then the sun, stooping
over the alleyway nursing a load

of lighted ice that the wind bevels
down to a peak that is almost a point

when I look: it might all have worked!
You might not have gotten involved in what ends

in your sweet, sweet rejection, Condensing
wind flows back into the world.

A World Written Down

Better off thinking of the mind as a postal system
in the service of the eyes. This at least would account

for the dominant shell-shocked look, like the street
when the winds blow so hard the air is papered

with cups and dressed up in straws. The local color
is the way trash always herds and collects at the foot

of the war memorial. The moral is
rain- and sleet-thickened wind is no pushover

but can beat so hard the eyeballs bug out and then
close like battered lunchstands. The result is the distant

gargantuan dumps, like Smashie's. He turns time into space,
too, pure space strung-out and mortgaged to the wind,

the huckster wind that owns everything. Stymied,
I review it, on the periphery of this city's

beloved archival endless featureless
print that's mortgaged no less to space and no less a mass plot

than a library. Fixed to a faraway clock is a wall,
the clock's like a little moon. Sadly they speak of hope,

lost hope, they ask out loud if it's proper
that they can talk out loud without hope and yet hope,

if it's clear they still believe in the mind
without thinking, if those without love can still love,

and how Federalism broke the single-authority thing
and agitated the outbreak from the fraternity

of equality and community and the subsequent tyranny
so mighty in all capitols that kills them each night

and artificially fucks them back into shape
in the morning or whenever they open their eyes

to cry softly, "The Old World is over," while they look
over the stacks for the clock. The wind comes along

just as I leave the building. It blows the doors open
and a hundred thousand books slam shut like lunchstands.

Noon

They talk these days like bigshots
as if only they can see
delicate coastlines in the curbs'
sweep, or the outlined unperturbed

morning in the dawn's lap
shedding the hours like tears
for the sun's departing
and the moon that loiters ahead

amid ten-penny stars. Like the heroes
hidden in their last names
or in the story of their deeds
they go ordering up a legend

we'll be told to put up with.
The rest of us will have to stay
tracing the unperturbable light
that's our Fatima

from this doggy, scrappy spot.
Yet remember the older version.
Common folk lived the stories out;
the bigshots got the credit.

Your grandmothers memorized coastlines
and walked them sunrise to sundown
crying for men who were ten years dead,
soldiers who never made it.

Somebody heard them crying from a blind spot
behind dunes the sun hits flush.

He remembered the tears for the bigshots
years later; he wrote them down.

Tears became spears, cries warcries,
the sullen women goddesses walking
forever and ever and ever across
less and less beach, each year.

Dazzling

Why couldn't it have stayed down there,
its first light running up and down
the alleys and tonguing the streets?
It just rose
as though, staggered by a blow from behind
and pushed through a door,
I had entered the wrong house.

Under the Blue Moon

(for Gellù Naum)

The plot is the disposition
of fossil bone in a ring of rope

and how the unguided child walked
abroad around a dark glass coastline

shoring off for good the world
he looked for. Under the moon

the monkeybars shone and the air
nibbled at summer's hard here-and-now

a thing at a time. The moon stamped
with a jet's geometry. By day

the science of being young displayed
like fossils beneath a vaulted roof

until the world in a museum filled
with boys seeking secrets. Everything was outside-in.

The giant bones on the flagstones tucked
their shadows away from the sun. The sky

stood for silence in the world
and the world stood whole in all its rooms—

the lots, the courts, the diamonds in
the cinderfields, the university museum—

where its objects' names were turned around
like streetsigns and the moon, that rat, went roaming.

And a door slammed.
The birds shrieked and pleated

an inhuman sun. The city
lit from above was a daydreamer startled

by sonic booming. The sun
combed heat waves out of the air

and harrowed the streets. The wind
chased the kids out of the sun. The door

locked and, lit and tossed at the world,
the sun burned down the horizon

and the moon turned blue.
For a long time all you could do was move

from room to room. Their disposition
was the pointless question

raised faithfully, like dust underfoot,
while in retreat. The prayers shaped

like charges rose up burning in escape
of earth's tangled shadow-woof. Lightning

flashed off the hipped roofs. The west,
all bloodshot with rain and sun-up, pressed

the sycamores to itself
decalled

on brick and blacktop. They loomed
like hired mourners tossing looks

over their shoulders, those trees
those spooky trees

There's a cry out back.

I want the cry out back, a brilliant
burst of noise from noise that stands out

nakedly, like taps. Tile is breaking.
The sound's carried to me raw on the wind,

not remixed into wounded mouthy marble,
just breaking tile

and sudden light. My open door
throws a mess of shadow down the steps

to the street
and the sun's scrutiny

while the kids on Mercy Street
war on the pigeons

cakewalking up on the roof. The kids run
raising their fists, sighting down their fingers

and the cannonade of slamming doors
behind them works even better.

The pigeons belch
and take off

settling in a building abandoned
on Seventh Street

for a while. Sighting down
one end of a day to its second or third

and so on is what is endless
so that noon is a second dawn, night a third

unless produced is some complete speech
accounting for the accounting, but you can't bluff

kids thrown back out in sunshine's finicky
pastures that things are settled. The old way,

that lies. It has to. When the lights went out
and breath escaped it went clear out of the house

of clay to where all the breaths dead ended,
the future's carrefour. The breath

got out with little more show than a man
touring an exhibition does

to get a drink or just time to mingle
or some fresh air. Voices

used to sneak through the silence and silence it
and the old situation, as it had to,

balanced like an equation. What a talk
yielded was distinct from the science

that backed it up, that fat reserve
of faithful inevitability

that made names money and quietness
careful scrutiny prior to purchasing

the last words, Gellù,
and breathlessness

and wonder. But the wind has blown that out
into the hurricane world.

                              This high-pitched wind,
each year, how much it recovers. The open vault

lets what goes on rehearse all forms
unbound, ceaselessly—

like the moon's ripple-effect in the clouds,
the sounds' full harmonic range is like light's

scattered organizations
no matter how high. The way shells

rattled under the wave that year
through the ocean's tonic and spelled a way

in, is how things are opened out—
a distant gratifying sonic boom,

the world is under weigh.
Right down there on the curb

light's shaken out of the gutter
like water out of a rainbow. And the high winds

are naked and plane and peel at the sky
but it stays up. This morning's wind

is sweet nothingness. The sky
for one instant's in a cup,

one beat too long exposed, too nakedly
reflexive, dark and dopey. Fixed

to a wish of fixity, the whole
fills with too-settled meanings

and a chaos of circles chopped up
and riding the upper lip

as the wind blows by and tips the cup.
The eyebrows that look like waves

aren't clouds but pigeons. Such stories
repeat on me.

                              In the end
the moon runs off who cares where,

in the gutter with blood and tapwater
in straightforward lines-of-sight that no more exist

than a faithful silence by itself.
A shrill note

burst out of the walls next door
like a public voice from a crowd

I've just run out of. Back there
the panes darkened by blue sky

it squats, battered jackass of hope
and sun that shines on the blinds,

the frames burst, the cornices chipped,
soffits sagging like balls, the standpipes

slumped and squashed like straws, the jambs
out of true and splayed into trapezoids, a window

as though screaming at me open and the door
shut on me spun around and gone

                              Now
in every sight unseen, singing
the song it sounds like you've sung

and talking the way around a boy
who fingered the ropes

under blue vaults, remember?
Through such a fastness of

what never got through
that roofless vault just

like a cartoon
reassembled from splinters

and the moon's blue bracelet
of ice-crystals comes in

tossed on the violent waters, the ring
at the bottom of things

that just fell out. *Keep*
and you shall find

the unfixed whole
unevenly initialed, like old

forms, seals the present.
The boy sneaks through fissured dawn

and quietly the horizontal
east owns everything.

The Contemporary Poetry Series

Edited by Paul Zimmer

The Contemporary Poetry Series

Edited by Bin Ramke

J. T. Barbarese, *Under the Blue Moon*
Wayne Dodd, *Sometimes Music Rises*
Gary Margolis, *Falling Awake*
Terese Svoboda, *All Aberration*